GW00600787

# Marrakech

*Fine living in riads*
*and "maisons d'hôtes"*

**Pascal Defraire**

is a photographer who has immortalised dozens of world landscapes on film; his aim is to share something of the character and soul of the places he visits. His photographs have illustrated many articles by Patricia Minne, and have appeared on the front covers of travel magazines on more than one occasion.

**Patricia Minne**

is a specialist journalist who has spent the last fifteen years criss-crossing the world, and has already published more than 60 major articles, some of which have earned her prizes from the international press. When visiting foreign countries, her approach is to seek out human contact and culture in all its varied forms, from art to architecture, taking in traditions and lifestyles on the way, and capture them – sometimes on film, but more often on paper (her first love is writing).

Layout: Sanny Chaudy.
Translation: Isalink.


14/1, rue de Paris
7500 Tournai (Belgium).
www.larenaissancedulivre.com

ISBN : 2-8046-0753-4

# Marrakech

*Fine living in riads and "maisons d'hôtes"*

Pascal Defraire
Patricia Minne

RENAISSANCE INTERNATIONAL

PALMERY
GUÉLIZ
HIVERNAGE
THE MEDINA
KASBAH
LAAROUSS
MOUASSIN
MELLAH (Jewish Quarter)
Majorelle Gardens
Cemetery
Place el Mourabiten
Bab Doukkala
Tourist Office
Place du 16 Novembre
Post Office
Rail way Station
Place de la Liberté
Bab er Raha
Bab Nkob
Law Courts
Bab el Makhzen
Casino
Bab el Jdid
La Mamounia
La Menara
Bab el Jdid Olivery
Route des Remparts
Bab el Khémis
Bab Kechiche
Sidi Bel Abbes mosque
Zaouïa de Sidi Ben Slimane el Jazouli
Riad Laila
Bab Doukkala Mosque
La Maison Arabe
Riad 72
Dar Moha
Dar el Glaoui (ou Dar el Bacha)
Riad Zina
Ben Youssef Mosque
Dyers' Souk
Ben Youssef Medersa
Place du Moukef
Mouassin Fountain
Spice sellers and apothecaries stalls
Dar Loubna
Riad Habib
Sidi Abd el Aziz Mausoleum
Mouassine Mosque
Sidi Moulay el KsourMosque
Riad Laksour
Craft centre
Place Jemâa el Fna
Koutoubia
Place Youssef Ben Tachfine
Villa des Orangers
Bab el Dabbagh
Tanneries
Bab Aylen
Bab Aghmat
Dar Si-Saïd
Bahia Palace
Riad Mabrouka
Place des Ferblantiers
Jewish Cemetery
El Mansour Mosque
El Badi Palace
Saadian tombs
Derb el Badii Mosque
Dar el Makhzen (Royal Palace)
Outer Mechouar
Bab Ahmar
Agdal Gardens
Grand Mechouar
Bab Ksiba
Bab Ighli
Bab er Robb
Sidi es Soheyli Mausoleum
Oued Issil
Palmery "Circuit"
Avenue Mohamed V
Avenue Yacoub el Mansour
Boulevard de Safi
Avenue Allah el Fassi
Avenue Hassan II
Avenue des Nations-Unies
Avenue du Président Kennedy
Avenue Moulay el Hassan
Avenue de Paris
Avenue de France
Avenue de la Menara
Avenue Houmman el Fetouaki
Avenue Bab el Jdid
Rue Bab Aghmat
Rue de Bab Ahmar
Rue de Bab Ighli
Rue de la Kasba
N
0 200 400 m
GÉOgraphisme
Renaissance International

# CONTENTS

It was at the foot of the High Atlas mountains, on the very edge of the desert, that the Almoravids founded the imperial city of Marrakech. A succession of periods of alternating grandeur and decadence filled it with sumptuous palaces, imposing mosques, sublime gardens and magnificent residences, protected by thick walls in the city colours: ochre and red, just like the fertile soils of the plain of Haouz.

Although history has not been kind to it – stripping it of its status as capital city and consigning its prosperity to the past – the Medina walls and the million trees of the Palmery ensure that this remains an extraordinary setting which can now be discovered by the privileged guests staying at the riads and small palaces, painstakingly renovated in the traditional way. They provide an opportunity to sample not only Moroccan cuisine – which forms an integral part of the local culture – but also the Marrakchi hospitality and lifestyle... and an astonishingly refined lifestyle at that!

# Marrakech
## *an imperial city*

Founded in 1062 by an Almoravid sultan who established his kingdom's capital there, Marrakech increased in wealth over the following dynasties, each adding to its luxury and prosperity. The Almohads gave it the Koutoubia mosque (the most beautiful in the city), and rebuilt the city itself, which was at the time filled with palaces. However, in the thirteenth century, when the Merinids deserted it for Fès, it was pillaged and entered a period of decline. This lasted for three centuries until the arrival of the Saadians, who bestowed many architectural treasures upon Marrakech: the now-ruined El Badi palace, and a number of *medersas*, mosques and fountains to adorn the city, which they also chose as the site for their tombs. However, the Alaouites repeated history by putting an end to this period of economic and cultural revival: they settled in Meknès and razed the El Badi palace to the ground. The only bright patch in this inglorious period of history was the reign of Sultan Moulay Hassan, who returned to the "red town", restoring its palaces, mosques and La Ménara, and giving the city one of the treasures of its heritage: the Bahia Palace.

From 1912 onwards, Marrakech was extricated from its economic slump by its French protectorate. A "new" town was grafted onto the Medina: Guéliz, which incorporates the Hivernage residential quarter and still forms the nucleus of the town's essential services, with its banks, official buildings, travel agencies, offices and hotels. But among the small buildings dating back to the 1930s-1950s, where most of the Europeans still live, concrete buildings have proliferated and extended the territory of Marrakech into new quarters. Wide boulevards now link the Medina to the airport and La Ménara, formerly isolated amid its vast gardens. But the *calèche* horse-drawn carriage (or the bicycle) is still the transportation method of choice for a tour of the Palmery "circuit" – a thin strip more than twenty kilometres in length, alternating between asphalt and sand as it winds its way through this immense 13,000 hectare estate. It traverses a desert planted with palm trees, passing the occasional hamlet apparently unaware of the existence of the town and the large estates hidden away inside their imposing walls. Shepherd-boys still bring their flocks to graze at the entrance to the Medina and the foothills of the High Atlas, whose snowy peaks carve out the backdrop to this setting.

Rabat may be the country's political capital, but Marrakech is its religious centre. King Mohammed VI, who is said to enjoy close links with his people, makes regular visits to the Royal Palace, built in the eighteenth century but fully restored by his father, Hassan II. More than 3,000 craftsmen were drafted in to turn this residence into a real jewel, which – unfortunately – remains closed to the public.

The Medina is the heart of Marrakech. It is said that one-fifth of Marrakchis live here, and that more than 65% of the remaining (active) population work here. They are divided into groups traders, labourers and craftsmen, with each group occupying its own location according to its trade... In this way, beyond the *quartiers*, one finds a multitude of souks, each with their groups of manufacturers and merchants: scrap metal dealers, ironworkers, dyers, tanners and jewellers... not to forget the merchants who particularly target tourists and sell spices, carpets, fabrics, leather goods and a range of variously genuine and fake antique souvenirs...

Boulevard Mohammed V, providing a connection to the new town via the front of the Craft centre, starts its journey at Place Jemâa-El-Fna, the true centre of the old town. Its dimensions are inversely proportional to the narrowness of the labyrinth of back-streets in the Medina, most of which are closed to traffic. The square has little beauty and even less charm, and throbs by day to the incessant rhythm of traffic: taxis of varying magnitude (just like the fares they charge) and overloaded buses. As night falls, the invasion begins... a casual, strolling army of Marrakchis and tourists alike, all in search of atmosphere, observed by hundreds of curious onlookers peering down from the heights of a terraced rooftop café as though they were manning lookout posts.

And then there are the palaces – some transformed into museums, others virtually in ruins – the out-of-bounds mosques, the often-elusive fountains amid the tangle of narrow lanes, and a handful of gardens. We will discover them over the course of the following pages, sandwiched between pairs of riads which also play a part in the architectural and cultural heritage of the city. For long years they have remained secret and intimate, for the eyes of one family only, behind their windowless walls, invisible to the passer-by.

PREVIOUS DOUBLE PAGE:
Probably constructed during the Almohad dynasty, the Menara Garden is a garden of a hundred or so hectares filled with olive trees. In its day, it probably already possessed the immense 30,000 m² irrigation lake designed to supply the water needed to irrigate the olive trees through an elaborate network of underground canals. At the end of the nineteenth century, this long-neglected green space was redeveloped, and a house with a green-tiled roof was built alongside the lake to accommodate the Sultan's extramarital activities. Today, it is open to the public, and Marrakchis come here to take early evening walks with family and friends, to enjoy the fresh air and watch the sun sinking into the water of the pool...

# The riads

## *a Garden of Eden in the Medina*

The houses used to belong – and in some cases still do belong – to rich Moroccan families. Heavy with several centuries of history, they have often been decorated by artists and craftsmen commissioned from all over the country to sculpt wood panelling, paint doors, carve columns and decorate the floors with multicoloured *zellij mosaics*... Many of these houses were gradually abandoned or neglected as the town declined and fortunes were reversed. Most of the houses which were transformed into *"maisons d'hôtes"* were either sold to Europeans or renovated by Moroccans with a love for this exceptional heritage, which continues to conceal its charms behind heavy doors and anonymous façades, away from prying eyes. Now restored in accordance with former traditions, more than two hundred riads – not all of which have been catalogued – play a significant part in the charm of Marrakech, whose ancestral way of life they reflect. This number will ultimately rise to three hundred or more, providing competition for the concrete hotels which have proliferated in Guéliz – the modern town – and the tourist-trap restaurants with precious little authenticity. To stay in a riad is to taste the subtle or (in some cases) opulent charm of another culture... to enjoy an individual welcome and the calm of a refuge hidden away at the heart of a labyrinth of backstreets buzzing with life.

A riad (the word literally means "garden", but is also used to mean "garden of Eden" is more than just a mere house. It is a reflection of many centuries of tradition; a particular social philosophy; a certain view of women; an expression of domestic Moroccan architecture or, at its simplest level, local culture.

With its combination of Arab and Andalusian themes and its extreme refinement, this family dwelling is designed according to very precise criteria, without which it cannot be a riad; rather, it it is a *dar*.

To qualify as a riad, a house must be built within the Medina, have at least two party walls and be constructed around a patio decorated with four planted or flower borders and a fountain or pool representing the heavenly garden and its vegetation or water, the source of life. However, although it was intended as a foretaste of paradise, with its exquisitely-worked *gap plasterwork*, doors and columns, long, draped wall-hangings and coloured cushions, the riad was also a gilded prison for women, who saw nothing of the world outside save for the sky and the roofs and terraces of the neighbouring houses.

There is only one doorway in the neglected façade, and no windows – not even barred windows – to provide even the slightest contact with the street outside, thus protecting the interior of the house from prying eyes and heat alike. A long, narrow corridor leads directly to the patio, surrounded by salons with no connecting doors between each other, acting as living rooms; it was here that guests were often received, or occasionally on long sofas in the shadows of the arcades, at low tables on which a silver teapot and carved, gold-rimmed glasses were placed. In one corner of the courtyard is the entrance to the kitchen, fairly small and above all functional.

The bedrooms and apartments are upstairs. A number of generations would sometimes share the riad, creating a real family community. The size depended on the family fortune, and some such dwellings had two or even three patios and many rooms, without sacrificing the intimate character providing so much of their charm.

Having been resold, restored and transformed, very few riads still retain all of their characteristic features. In some cases, fountains have been replaced by swimming pools; while in others, pots of flowers may now take the place of the flowerbeds and trees which continue to surround the patios of other riads. The oldest of the residences have also required the installation of running water and electricity, which were not always originally provided. And many such dwellings were simply abandoned after a number of generations, marriages and deaths, or the departure of the children to explore fresh horizons in another town... or another country...

# *Riad 72*

72 is simply the house's number, printed in giant figures above the entrance doorway, squatting anonymously at the end of a narrow lane in the Medina. Here as elsewhere, the doorway is set into a windowless wall with very little to recommend it to the passer-by. And yet it opens onto an astonishing "maison d'hôtes" which has been the subject of a number of articles in international interior design magazines. It is fair to say that this beautiful riad, decorated in the matching blacks, reds and whites of a minimalist design combining elements of Zen with Arab references, is a one-of-a-kind example. Its Italian owner has turned it into a small bijou residence which is modern yet traditional, while remaining faithful to the house's original structure and design philosophy. Contemporary furniture rubs shoulders with antiques and the inevitable Moroccan lanterns, while the patio has been transformed into an enormous salon, refreshed by a modern, high-tech reinterpretation of the long pool beneath the leaves of high banana trees. Upstairs, a superb suite and three bedrooms sit alongside a combined library and salon which opens onto a gallery with a matting-covered floor. *Tadlakt* (polished lime plaster) dominates the bathrooms, some of whose baths take the unexpected form of huge, square vats. A staircase leads to the terrace-solarium, with the refreshment of a small pool and a canopy-covered rest area affording one of the finest views to be found anywhere in Marrakech...

72

# Marrakech

## *The souks of the Medina*

Marrakech's souk is at least as old as the town itself, and is said to be the largest in Morocco. The simple stalls have given way to workshops and permanent shop structures, arranged in a maze of lanes which, despite initial appearances, conform to an almost uniform plan. Each trade group has its own "quarter", sited according to its former prestige or importance – starting at the centre, which was traditionally considered to be the prime location. Today, this structure is tending to dissolve, but it still generally holds true that, say, ironworkers will not be found alongside sellers of carpets or spices.

The souks, combining a business and social function, are more than just a permanent market or glorified bazaar for tourists. They also act as a meeting place where Marrakchis come to exchange gossip, conduct business or just stroll beneath the reed matting which covers most of the streets.

Each souk has its own atmosphere, colours and smells; and these are not always pleasant, as for example in the case of the tanners, whose vats give off noxious aromas which are sure to repel the casual observer. Even so, their quarter is just as interesting and photogenic as that of the dyers, with its skeins of multicoloured wool drying in the sun, suspended across the thoroughfares on washing lines or hanging from walls and doorways.

Further away from the tourist alleys near Place Jemâa-El-Fna, the ironworkers' souk resounds to the clang of hammer on metal, fashioning lamps, chairs, screens, tables and other sundry decorative or everyday objects. A little further on, craftsmen are working wood and palm fibres into *chouaris*, the double baskets placed on donkeys' backs, from which this busy souk takes its name. The *kisarias* (cedar-roofed galleries) are reserved for fabric merchants, and superb brocades and other precious materials can still be found here. Further to the north, in the carpet souk, an auction (better known in these parts as the *criée berbère*, or Berber auction) is also held at around four in the afternoon. And gradually, you lose yourself in this labyrinth, with the occasional insistent interruption by a loquacious merchant along the way. You stop for a relaxed mint tea, which requires more bargaining. And if you're lucky enough to be the first customer of the day, you may be given an extra-special deal, as dictated by custom... and superstition...

# Riad Zina

Beate Prinz is a German-born mother of three children with a training in weaving. Having run a farm in the Alpes-Maritimes for twenty years, she came to settle in Morocco where, as she says, she particularly enjoys the local friendliness, the colour of the sky and the feeling that there's always plenty of time, despite the long working hours. Love at first sight compelled her to buy and redecorate a riad built a little over 350 years ago at the heart of the Medina, not far from the picturesque ironworkers' quarter.

There was a time when the Medina was inhabited mainly by civil servants and wealthy families. After several successive generations of inheritance, this riad – which used to be much larger – was divided into three sections. The previous owners of the section bought by Beate had lived there for nearly forty years. The property had been shared by up to fifteen people, but when the children married and moved away from home, the house became too big and too much work for the parents to look after.

Beate kept the original room structure, but was obliged to renovate completely, not least because the building had neither water nor electricity. She opted for sober minimalism, and thus removed the mosaics, although without sacrificing the local colour: the decorative objects are either Moroccan or picked up as travel souvenirs, and most of the furniture – stainless steel, wood and leather – was made in the Medina.

While the bedrooms have plenty of charm of their own, the immense Al Kamar suite on the first floor (50 m$^2$!) is quite simply magic. It is sober yet very Oriental, with its red satin pouffes, *kilim* rugs and coloured silk blankets. In the patio, which is set into relief by an adorable pool with rose petals floating on the surface, a small library on the sofa in the *bouhou* (outdoor salon) entices you to stop and read for a moment. It is a calm and very pleasant place, offering an exotic, comfortable and well-located bed and breakfast arrangement near the Medersa, the Koranic school and Marrakech museum.

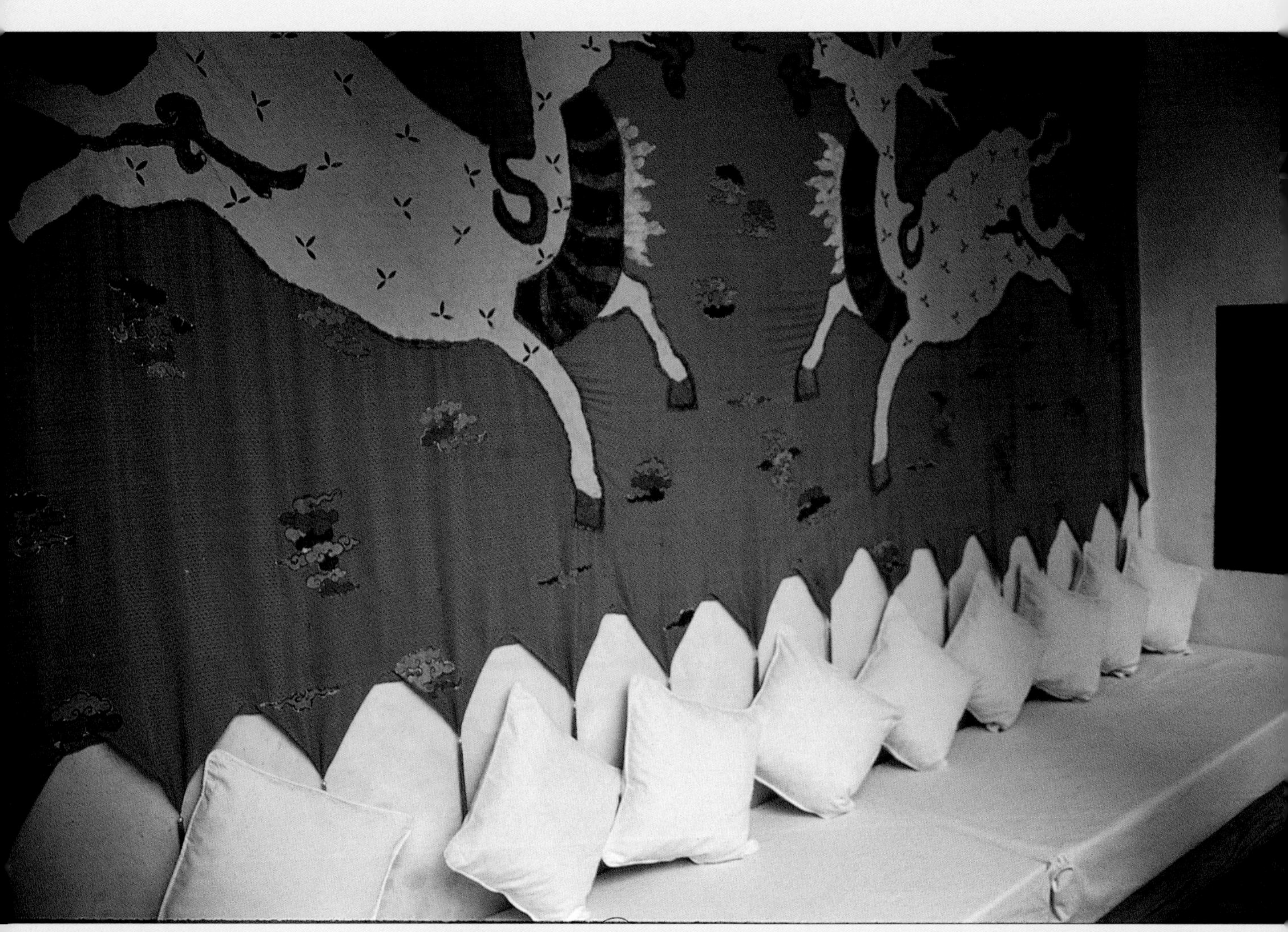

Plantes médicinales
Land
GEO

# Riad Laksour

Very close to the Place Jemâa-El-Fna, the Laksour riad is hidden away behind the walls of a lane in the souks, whose frantic activity seems simply to pass it by. Ahmed ben Cherki, its Moroccan proprietor, is a specialist in renovating these old residences: he has fashioned a career from it, and has thus made many a contribution to the renaissance of this exceptional local heritage.

Ahmed ben Cherki has preserved the original charm of the Laksour riad, with its many nooks and crannies and its string of rooms arranged around two patios, one of which has a large pool. The wholly Oriental decoration adds a touch of exoticism and refinement. Upstairs are two suites with *zouaqué* (painted wood) ceilings, and warm-coloured *gaps* decorate the walls, sometimes set back into alcoves.

More than any of the other riads visited, Laksour jealously guarded its women from the public gaze. The patio is surrounded not by floors of terraces, but by walls set with grilled windows on three sides, making it possible to see without being seen. From the terrace, the vista stretches as far as the High Atlas and takes in Place Jemâa-El-Fna, the Koutoubia and the Medina roofs.

With its original mosaics, hundred-year-old-plus doors, richly-covered hangings, carpets, tinted glass tiles, pouffes and Moroccan antiques, the Laksour riad has remained authentic, discreet and intimate, with staircases which are so narrow that it is often impossible for two people to pass. It is a place full of charm and hospitality in which two suites and three bedrooms cohabit the same space without ever drawing guests' attention to the fact they are sharing…

This riad used to be the house of a vizir who owned six adjacent houses – veritable palaces which in fact lent the quarter its name (Laksour means "palace").

CAFE

# Marrakech

## *Place Jemâa-El-Fna*

On Place Jemâa-El-Fna in the evening, the merchants' stalls, improvised snacks of grilled chicken, meat kebabs or fish, snake charmers, acrobats, story-tellers and... pickpockets continue the ballet begun by the buses, taxis, bicycles, cart-pulling donkeys and pedestrians, attracting a strolling crowd consisting of Marrakchis and tourists, who also fill the terraces on the café roofs, just like the boxes in a theatre showing the same play day after day, under the reddish lighting of the setting sun.

And yet this esplanade, along which sultans from a bygone era used to display the heads of the executed, is of interest only for its ability to metamorphose at various different times of the day. It is still possible to find a few water-carriers, whose presence owes more to folklore than to utility (whatever you do, don't drink their water), and who rely on tourists for their daily income – they never pose for photographs for free!

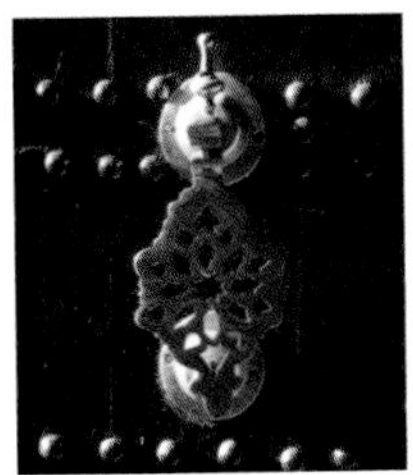

# Villa des Orangers

Built in 1940, this house used to belong to a Marrakchi of some note and was bought by a French couple who discovered it while travelling. The story goes that it took them only one night to make up their minds, but nine months to carry out the renovation work which transformed this superb riad into a charming five-star hotel with membership of the international Relais et Châteaux chain.

*Zellij* (mosaics), marbles, sculpted wood panelling and *tadlakt*, all created and fitted by local craftsmen, make this a little architectural and decorative jewel, faithful to Moroccan tradition. The ground was redeveloped with mixed earth, which was then pressed down before finally being smoothed off with wooden spatulas and covered with cement, into which a multitude of tiles were inset. This *bejmat* (as it is known) covers 1,600 m$^2$, adding sculptured *gaps* and ancient painted doors to the oriental atmosphere. In the bathrooms, the walls are decorated with wrought columns and the basins are in the shape of bowls.

However, despite the luxury and beauty of the décor, it still has the intimacy of a riad, with its tree-lined patios (orange trees, in this case) and small salons. On the roof, a pool serves as a swimming pool and a few bedrooms have private terraces. To round it all off, the Villa des Orangers is a stone's throw from the Koutoubia mosque, Place Jemâa-El-Fna is not far away, and the warmth of the welcome matches the discretion and quality of the service – without forgetting the decoration, which is in no way flashy but instead in excellent taste.

# The Kasbah

While the souks, the Koutoubia and the Place Jemâa-El-Fna may be the best-known and most frequently-visited areas of the Medina, the old town, delimited by its walls, has many other curiosities to offer which are hard to spot from within the tangle of narrow streets. From the tops of the terraces, the eye sees only flat roofs punctuated by the square minarets of the mosques or the (also square) tower of a palace. Against the horizon are silhouetted the High Atlas mountains, provided they are not hidden by a heat haze – which they often are in summer.
South of Place Jemâa-El-Fna, Dar Si Saïd – the former vizir's palace – is now home to the Museum of Moroccan Arts and Crafts, and is worth a visit as much for the building itself as for its contents. A little further on, in the kasbah – the fortified section of the town – the ruins of the opulent Saadian tombs (sixteenth century) rub shoulders with those of the El Badia palace (end of the sixteenth century), of which nothing remains save an esplanade, pools, underground galleries, a pavilion and sections of walls in which storks now nest. Although these vestiges retain an air of majesty, they give little idea of the former splendour of this "Palace of the Incomparable", which had 360 rooms arranged around a vast courtyard containing a pool 90 metres long by 20 metres wide! It took 25 years of labour to complete this masterpiece, and the Alaouite Moulay Ismaïl was very careful to remove the finest treasures to his palace in Meknès before ordering its destruction… The current Royal Palace adjoins the El Badi palace, and is closed to the public. Along its eastern edge, beyond the kasbah, runs the *mellah* (the Jewish quarter) and its maze of small streets squeezed between the Bahia Palace to the north and the Agdal Gardens, forming a haven of tranquillity amid a city in perpetual motion. Built by the Saadians in the sixteenth century to house the Jewish community, the mellah's inhabitants are now mainly Muslim, but the quarter retains its covered market, selling shoes, clothing and other textiles, and costume jewellery, but also spices, aromatic herbs and any number of remedies and old wives' favourites – such as walnut bark, which makes an effective replacement for toothpaste.

# *Dar Moha*

The door to this apparently ordinary house leads out into a fairly wide road which is open to traffic. It looks rather like the door to a restaurant, which in fact is precisely what this *dar* is, as well as being a "maison d'hôtes". With its patio and four garden borders arranged around a fountain, this former residence of the secretary of the Pacha Glaoui, built in the nineteenth century and later bought by the French fashion designer Pierre Balmain as a secondary residence, met the necessary criteria for a riad. A number of modifications were then made: a swimming pool (installed on the huge patio), en-suite bathrooms added to the three bedrooms, each of which bears the name of a colour (green, yellow and red), and the décor, which has been revised in accordance with Balmain's highly Art Deco tastes. Most of the items which furnish the *dar* are taken from the personal collection of the designer himself; he sold them as part and parcel of the house when health problems prevented him from coming to stay at the property.

The Dar Moha is now owned by a Moroccan chef, Moha Fedal, who has therefore given a higher priority to themed salons in which refined meals are served in sometimes surprising settings which are imbued with the memory of their decorator. The Marrakchi lifestyle is now focused mainly on the courtyard, around the swiming pool, where cushions placed on the carpets await guests at tea time. In another corner, tables with pink cloths, matching the *zellij* mosaics which constitute the frieze on the wall, enjoy the shade of the trees pointing straight up towards the sky. This is a fine place to come for a mint tea or a lamb *tagine*...

# Marrakech

## *The Koutoubia*

Built by the Almohads (twelfth century), the Koutoubia is the main mosque in Marrakech. Entry is forbidden to non-Muslims (as with all other mosques), and so it should be admired from the outside, which is fairly sober – like the façades of the palace. After all, in Morocco, luxury was reserved for the interior, richly decorated from floor to ceiling in order to impress guests.

The main feature of the Koutoubia is its minaret, the only surviving part of a previous mosque which was destroyed almost immediately upon completion because of its incorrect alignment in relation to Mecca. Completed more than twenty years after the inauguration of the mosque, this sixty-nine-metre high square tower was used as a model for Seville's Giralda, and is considered to be one of the finest Islamic minarets anywhere. Each of its faces was decorated in a different way, and its six interior rooms, each with its arched windows, are stacked one on top of the other, topped by a terrace and dome, whose copper arrow adds eight metres to the height of the edifice.

# *Dar Loubna*

At the heart of the souks and the Mouassine quarter, Dar Loubna is a tiny house; simple, laid out like a riad, but too modest to qualify as one of these small, sumptuously-decorated palaces. The white walls, the décor (which is minimalist, but typically local in colour), the courtyard and its *zellij*-covered fountain all make this a real haven of peace and coolness. Long wall hangings provide shade for the upstairs galleries, surrounding the patio on three sides like balconies around a theatre stage on which a new scene of life is acted out daily. The roof terrace overlooks the terraces of neighbouring houses and also the Medina, in this ancient palace quarter with its sunset colours...

# *Riad Habib*

A few minutes away from the previous residence, Riad Habib was bought and restored by a Marrakchi hotelier who planned to give it a distinctly elegant touch. The entrance door opens onto a long, richly-decorated corridor which leads to a small patio shaded by high palm trees fanning the upstairs gallery and its reading room.

Although the salon furniture may be a little overblown, the bedrooms, the courtyard and its wall fountain with ochre and blue *zellij* mosaics are more authentically Moroccan. On the first floor is a suite with a mezzanine level, while on the roofs, the terrace holds a surprise in store. With its pergola, *zellij* tables and forged iron chairs with their soft cushions, it offers its own unbeatable view across the Medina, the Koutoubia, the High Atlas and the neighbouring riads...

MAISON
D'HOTE

# Marrakech

## *The Mouassine quarter and the Medersa*

The Mouassine quarter is one of the most attractive anywhere in the Medina. It can also boast a pretty mosque (not open to visitors), a superb fountain and the most interesting through route to the Marrakech Museum – located inside the beautiful nineteenth-century Dar M'Nebhi palace – and the Medersa ben Youssef, by way of the dyers' souk, the Souk Chouari (carpentry), and the souks of the copper-workers, slipper-makers and blacksmiths, with a possible detour via the instrument-makers' souk and a pause outside the Ba'Adiyn *koubba* (mausoleum), the only remaining trace of the Almoravids left standing in Marrakech, thanks to frequent restoration work over the years.

A *medersa* is a Koranic school which accompanies a mosque and is open to the public. The original Youssef medersa was built in the fourteenth century, but the current building – which can accommodate up to nine hundred students – dates from the sixteenth century and was one of the most important institutions in North Africa. Particular attractions are its marble-floored courtyard, surrounded by arches, decorated in sculpted plaster and cedarwood, blue and turquoise-toned mosaics and a washbasin for performing ablutions. There is also the prayer room, dimly lit by twenty or so small openings carved, lace-like, into the stucco…

Continuing eastwards towards the Bab ed-Debbagh (one of the Medina gates), one reaches the tanners' quarter, perhaps the furthest away from the residential areas, which are therefore spared the odour of skins and soaking vats which it generates. However, if you can put up with the smell, the spectacle of craftsmen at work is an impressive one, and worth a detour to see.

Near the Bab Fteuh (south of Rue Mouassine), the quarter is also home to many *fondouks* and *caravanserais*, the forerunners of the modern-day traveller's motel. The caravan-drivers stayed in the upstairs sections, built around a large central court reserved for the animals. Today, the *fondouks* are used for storing merchandise, and are homes to bazaars and antique dealers.

# *Riad Laïla*

If it is true that the riad reflects the fortune or social standing of its owner, the owner of this riad must be rich... very rich. For this dwelling has the size and appearance of a veritable small palace built more than two centuries ago, in several locations which probably originally formed two houses. The first part is built around two sides of an immense 240 $m^2$ patio, at the centre of which is a pool which is in every respect a swimming pool, in the shade of fruit and palm trees. A vast living area is spread out under the arcades of a *bouhou* (outdoors salon). Its superb, refined painted wooden doors with their blue and gold tones are original fittings. Most of the bedrooms and suites overlook the more modest (but still charming) patio of a *douirrya* (small adjoining house). Large white hangings have been suspended beneath the upstairs arcades, providing both shade and intimacy. The large terraces on the roofs have been made into rest and dining areas, and a Berber tent contains a salon and several low tables. It is an ideal place to enjoy a cup of tea, along with the view of the High Atlas and the minarets of the Medina.

# Riad Mabrouka

Right next to the Bahia palace, and a stone's throw from the mellah – the old Jewish quarter – this large riad seems every bit as princely. It was restored to fit in with its neighbours by a young Belgian architect, while the owner concentrated on the décor, combining "comfort and discreet luxury", a Moroccan or colonial style and Art Deco influences in vast amounts of space, refreshed by corner fountains and a beautiful pool nestling against one of the patio walls.

The bedrooms are concealed behind the ground floor arcades, beneath the columned galleries of the first floor or around a small, private adjoining patio with a traditional *bouhou* and a fountain. An antechamber has been turned into a place for reading, and the great terrace has an external salon beneath a canopy, a solarium and small corners for relaxation in which food is also served. Once again, the panoramic view takes in the Bahia quarter and the whole Medina...

# Marrakech

## *The Bahia Palace*

The Bahia palace, from which the surrounding quarter takes its name, was built in the late nineteenth century for the Grand Vizir of the sultan of the day, then extended over the following decades. Sober and refined, it displays its ceilings in painted and sculpted cedar, sumptuous reception rooms and patios filled with trees and flowers, without forgetting the superb marble courtyard of the harem with its fountain centrepiece and surrounding bedrooms for the concubines.

An unusual feature of this palace is that nearly all of the rooms are on the ground floor: for it is said that the Grand Vizir was short and overweight, and preferred to avoid the inconvenience of stairs…

# The Maison Arabe

Built in the late nineteenth century, this old family house was made into a famous restaurant in the 1930s, welcoming the likes of Churchill and Paul Bowles before closing its doors for nearly fifteen years, and then at last being sold and converted into a charming hotel by Fabrizio Ruspoli, a lover of architecture, music and gardens. French, but with an Italian father, he made regular visits to his grandmother, a Tangier-based archaeologist: he fell in love with the country and decided in the 1990s to settle here. He restored and decorated this double riad, using Moroccan furniture and local materials, drawing heavily upon *tadlakt* and cedar panelling. It took the Marrakchi craftsmen fully two years to create its current and undeniably luxurious appearance.

Within a stone's throw of the walls of Guéliz and the business quarter, it now contains about ten rooms and a highly-reputed restaurant around a nucleus of two courtyards, providing the sort of comfort one would expect from a luxury hotel.

The Maison Arabe also has a garden (and a large swimming pool), outside the Medina. There is a shuttle bus for customers, who can also take introductory lessons in Moroccan cooking in the country's first culinary school. All of these make this fashionable address a refined illustration of many aspects of fine living, Marrakech-style...

# Marrakech

## *The city walls*

Constructed in the twelfth century by the Almoravids before being further expanded by the Almohads and the Saadians, Marrakech's city walls run for nearly twenty kilometres around the Medina and include around two hundred square towers. Built from clay and lime adobe, and red in colour like the town itself, they are thick (up to two metres), with ten or so gates or *babs*, some of which are truly remarkable. Bab Agnaoui is one such example, in the fortified quarter of the Kasbah and the Saadian tombs. The best-preserved section runs along the edge of Hivernage, west of the Medina.

The panoramic view of the snowy peaks of the High Atlas afforded from here is particularly photogenic at sunset…

# "Maisons d'hôtes" in the Palmery

*"Once upon a time, there was a fertile plain: Haouz, at the foot of the High Atlas. When the conqueror Youssef ben Tachfine arrived with his troops, he decided to set up camp there. They were carrying so many dates as provisions that, from the discarded fruit stones, a multitude of date palm trees grew..."* According to legend at least, this is the origin of the Palmery...

Real little palaces can be found amid the vast oasis-like surroundings of the Palmery, far from the walls of the Medina and the noise of the town. A number of these have also been converted into "maisons d'hôtes", decorated with luxury and refinement, surrounded by a garden which, out here in the desert, appears nothing short of a miracle. They provide a dreamy, exotic environment, and would furnish enough material on their own for a wonderful book on décor.

Regardless of what the legends say, the Palmery is a natural forest which is now being threatened by the proliferation of luxury residences, whose owners prefer the peace and quiet of the surrounding area to the bustle and stifling heat of the town. Lack of maintenance of the *khettara* irrigation channels has also damaged the irrigation system and killed a large number of trees. There has thus been a spread of small-scale farming and animal grazing in the bare areas, gradually taking its toll on the original vegetation. However, although the palm trees are becoming rarer in places, the area remains impressive in general, and it is easy to see why the rich come here to escape the noise and lack of space of the city, a short walk from the golf clubs which have also sprung up here.

# *Jnane Tamsna*

At the heart of the Palmery, the sublime Jnane Tamsna is a recent creation by Meryanne Loum-Martin, who already owns the Dar Tamsna (a collection of villas for rent) and the Riad Tamsna – which contains shops, a restaurant, a tea room and a series of temporary exhibitions – in the Medina.

Jnane Tamsna has the appearance both of a riad transplanted from its original setting and of a large family country house, decorated with sepia photographs, furniture, curios and old carpets which look as if they have been handed down from generation to generation. This talented Senegal-born decorator, married to an American anthropologist, has created a combination of comfort, prestige and elegance in decorating this two-patio house, both with Moroccan antiques and with furniture which she designed herself and commissioned from local craftsmen. The bedrooms are themed in a range of yellows, ochre, beiges, reds and browns, and have an extremely refined character. Outside, a long swimming pool with (heated) turquoise water extends along a six-hectare garden planted with hundred-year-old palms, olive trees, wild herbs and four organic vegetable gardens.

A former lawyer at the Paris Bar, Meryanne Loum-Martin turned her back on her profession to devote her full time to her passion for architecture, history and decorative arts. She now offers holidays themed around healthy cooking and a Mediterranean "fusion", but also an introduction to Moroccan culture and crafts, and local traditions regarding the use of plants.

Although the property may not have the sheen of the old family riads, it has the advantage of a well-lit setting with easy access both to the patios and to a ground-floor terrace, which most certainly adds to its individual character. It should also be noted that the property includes four other "maisons d'hôtes" which increase its capacity to a total of thirty rooms, for hire as a block or individually.

# Dar Ayniwen

A sandy track stops in front of a high enclosing wall with a heavy wooden door. As you pass through, you enter another world... a paradise in the middle of the desert. The villa – a real little palace – is not far from the entrance and, from the steps, the heavenly setting is already visible: an immense park, a swimming pool, a house (which has also been converted into a "maison d'hôtes") and a veritable botanical garden with a paved path through the centre of it, between lawns, exotic plants, hundred-year-old trees, an Andalusian pool filled with papyrus, water lilies and goldfish, fountains, pavilions and other places of pleasure.

The residence, built in 1980, originally housed a two-child family and "lots of friends" before its conversion to a "villa-hotel" with a number of suites and some more recent rooms – all of which have, however, been traditionally decorated. The furniture combines oriental, colonial and retro styling; the Moroccan and European antiques are either original family property or brought back from Jacques Abtan's travels – his son Stéphane now runs the estate. Each item has its own history, even in the bathrooms with their marble and mosaic-covered walls and floors, which are in some cases packed with impressive collections of bottles. Here, all is luxury and refinement, even in the kitchen itself, where food is served on silver plates. A world of tradition in a villa-museum which combines stylish living and modern comfort...

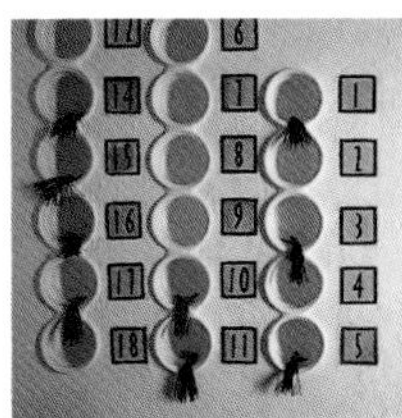

# Caravan Serai

After having decorated so many hotels and riads, the Moroccan-born architect and designer Charles Boccara – assisted in decorative matters by the Briton Max Laurence – has created a magnificent "maison d'hôtes", designed – after the fashion of a riad – around a patio enclosed within four walls. However, the terraces open outwards, and are in some cases private and self-contained, as are the pools belonging to two of the suites, sitting like two mini-riads at the centre of the vast property.

Unlike other similar properties, the Caravan Serai is sited at the edge of a small village on the outskirts of the Palmery, in an estate which was built in 1950 and formerly housed two families. Few modifications have been made, with most of the work focusing on a restoration of the décor without modifying the original architecture. However, a real swimming pool has taken the place of the fountain in the centre of the patio, separated from the rest of the courtyard by two enormous drapes suspended in mid-air.

Here, the decoration tends towards sobriety rather than palatial luxury. The terracotta, the woven carpets and blankets, the dark wood fashioned into artisanal chairs, chests and tables, the bamboo wardrobes, the adobe walls and ceilings... everything is reminiscent of the rural Moroccan style typical of the Marrakech region, as well as a number of features inspired by the Rif mountain range, or a vast Berber encampment, comfortable and refined. A surprise-filled setting for lovers of exoticism and total tranquility...

# *Les Deux Tours*

Set in more than three hectares of oasis, Les Deux Tours can boast six "maisons d'hôtes" decorated by its co-owner Charles Boccara, in the shadow of their own private enclosing wall. He has used generous quantities of adobe, terracotta, *tadlakt* and *zellij* mosaics in decorating these villas, each with a patio garden, a small private swimming pool, first floor terraces, a salon with a fireplace and between three and five rooms and suites, just like the riads of the Medina. They can be hired in a block or as individual entities, and currently total twenty-four rooms (other accommodation is currently being prepared), each one tastefully decorated and distinctive, illustrating "a blend of cultures" and the slightly retro *ambiance* of furniture which is more Art Deco than Arab, although the basic concept is intended to echo a fourteenth-century Andalusian village.

In the gardens, where olive trees intermingle with orange and palm trees, a large swimming pool has been installed in the middle of a lawn, in front of a little knot of tables belonging to a small restaurant shaded by a roof and long drapes. A beautiful, traditional *hammam* steam bath is decorated with *zellij* mosaics, making its own contribution to the exotic atmosphere of this charming, tranquil property six kilometres from the centre of Marrakech.

# Marrakech cuisine

At a first glance, Marrakech cuisine is not dissimilar to the food enjoyed in other Moroccan towns. And while there may be a number of more typically local dishes, the main difference lies in the method of preparing the various different recipes, so that one prune *tagine* will never be identical to any other. The female *dadas* (older cooks with experience) pass on their culinary secrets to the young helpers who, in their turn, will later train other apprentices. In this way, recipes endure from generation to generation, forming a sort of gastronomic heritage which gives Moroccan cuisine more richness, flavour and diversity than is often imagined. It has been enriched by many diverse influences, conveyed by women from all over Africa – some as slaves, some as concubines – or by travelling merchants in some *fondouk* of the Medina. It has diversified from family to family, as different unions are made, creating a melting pot of culture and tradition. For in Morocco, cooking is intimately linked with life itself and its myriad of events: a *sellou* (a pyramid of flour mixed with roasted and then ground almonds) is prepared to revive the strength of women who have just given birth and are preparing for breastfeeding, a *tfaïa*, with almonds and hard eggs, is a traditional dish for newlywed husbands, a *herbel* (crushed wheat with milk) is consumed on New Year's day, and a *harira* (soup made from tomatoes and other vegetables, sometimes enlivened with a little meat) on the evenings of Ramadan, accompanied by a *sellou* and *griouchs* (shortbread)...

As for the many different traditional *tagines*, the chicken with candied lemon, the ubiquitous Berber or royal couscous dishes, with meat or vegetables... almost every family has "its own" recipe, which varies depending on the type and/or proportion of the spices used, the cooking method and the utensils, which can be made from terracotta, metal, wood, copper, wicker and sometimes even leather.

Sometimes the most seemingly simple dishes, such as the mixed salads, require several hours of preparation, while the tagines and couscous – once the ingredients have been measured, cut up or poured out – cook "on their own", but subsequently require considerable final decoration time. After all, Moroccans also "eat with their eyes", and when it is properly prepared, the food is not only delicious, but extremely photogenic too...

## Eating Moroccan-style

Although traditions are gradually giving way to the Western way of life, many Marrakchi families continue to eat Moroccan-style, sitting on cushions or sofas around low, round tables. There will be a succession of dishes, starting with hot and cold mixed salads, *briouats*, a *pastilla* of pigeons with almonds, then a tagine, often followed by a couscous before the dessert, consisting of a milk *pastilla* or fruit, eaten before mint tea is served with dry biscuits and cornes de *gazelle* (crescent-shaped Moroccan pastries), stuffed with delicious marzipan.

The dishes are arranged at the centre of the table, and diners fill their plates directly using a piece of Moroccan bread and three fingers of the right hand, in accordance with certain rules of propriety: hands must be washed in hot water poured from a sort of teapot over a copper basin which is passed from guest to guest; everyone must then wait until the master of the house declares that the meal may start.

Traditionally speaking, no wine, beer or any other alcoholic drink is consumed. This means that a bottle of wine is hardly the ideal present to offer one's hosts if you are invited to dinner.

In any case, alcohol is not available within the Medina proper. Fruit juices and tea, but more commonly water – sometimes flavoured – are the standard accompaniments to meals, which, according to the most basic rules of Moroccan hospitality, must never leave guests hungry...

Not very far from the Place Jemâa-El-Fna, in the Place Rahba Kdina, slaves were still being sold up until 1912. Since then, the square has been turned into a grain market, and is still home to the spices souk, one of the most popular tourist destinations. Almost adjacent, the apothecaries' stalls offer an infinite selection of traditional spices, as well as aromatic and medicinal herbs. These are often reputed to have aphrodisiac properties. Other offerings include dried chameleons and coral powder which are claimed to be an effective treatment for heart problems... without forgetting Moroccan Viagra, of course, which comes with a guarantee of "total effectiveness"...

# *A few recipes…*

# Kefta briouats (recipe from The Maison Arabe)

Briouats are small envelopes of ouarka (a very fine flaky pastry: see the recipe for milk *pastilla*), folded into triangles, rectangles or rolls and stuffed (in this case with minced meat known as *kefta*), before immersion in boiling oil.

**Ingredients for 50 pieces**

- 500 g minced meat,
- 50 sheets of ouarka (1 per briouat),
- 6 eggs,
- 150 g butter,
- 3 teaspoons cinnamon,
- 1 teaspoon coriander,
- 1 pinch pepper or strong chilli powder,
- 2 teaspoons mild chilli powder,
- salt,
- 1 onion.

Mix the minced meat with the coriander, salt, mild and strong chilli powder and the onion (chopped into small pieces), then fry it in a pan with the butter, stirring constantly until the juice evaporates. Next, gradually add the beaten eggs and cinnamon, continuing to stir for 3-4 minutes.

Put the stuffing into the centres of the ouarka sheets, and then fold or roll them. Fry in oil just a few minutes before serving. For a stronger "sweet and sour" taste, you can sprinkle the briouats with icing sugar or even ground cinnamon...

# Mixed salads

## Caramelised tomatoes (recipe from The Maison Arabe)

**Ingredients for 2 servings** (or 4 servings if part of a three-course meal, excluding dessert)

- 2 kg tomatoes,
- salt,
- 1 teaspoon cinnamon,
- 2 tablespoons sugar,
- 1 tablespoon sunflower or peanut oil,
- 1 tablespoon sesame seeds, for a final garnish.

Cut the tomatoes in half and remove the part containing the seeds. Cut up the remainder into a pressure cooker or large pot and add the salt and oil, then leave to simmer over a low heat for around an hour. At the end of cooking, pour in the powdered sugar and cinnamon until a lightly caramelised paste is obtained. Place at the centre of a bowl and garnish with the sesame seeds. These caramelised tomatoes can be served warm or cold.

# Diced courgette salad

**Ingredients for 2 servings**

- 500 g courgettes (with skins),
- 2 cloves garlic,
- 1 small bunch parsley,
- salt,
- 1 teaspoon cumin,
- 1 teaspoon lemon juice,
- 2 tablespoons olive oil.

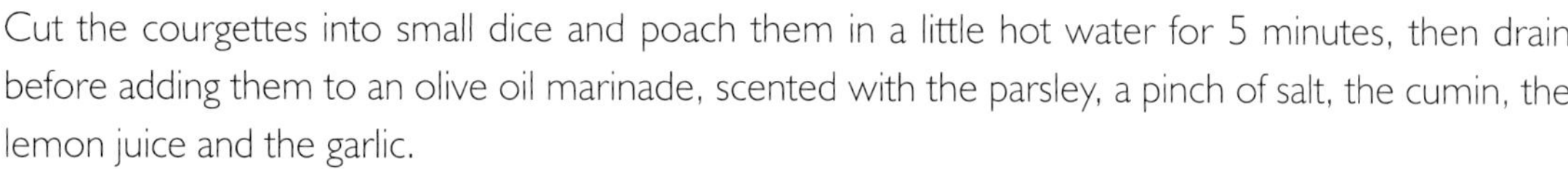

Cut the courgettes into small dice and poach them in a little hot water for 5 minutes, then drain before adding them to an olive oil marinade, scented with the parsley, a pinch of salt, the cumin, the lemon juice and the garlic.

Garnish the plate with a little parsley and orange slices.

# Diced turnip salad (recipe from The Maison Arabe)

**Ingredients for 2 servings**

- 500 g turnips,
- 2 cloves garlic,
- 1 small bunch parsley,
- salt,
- 1 teaspoon cumin,
- 1 teaspoon lemon juice,
- 2 tablespoons olive oil.

The preparation method is identical to the previous recipe in all respects. Garnish with parsley and a round slice of lemon.

# White cabbage salad (recipe from The Maison Arabe)

**Ingredients for 2 servings**

- 1 white cabbage heart,
- 2 cloves garlic,
- 1 small bunch parsley,
- salt,
- 1 teaspoon cumin,
- 1 teaspoon lemon juice,
- 2 tablespoons olive oil.

Cut the cabbage into strips and poach them for 5 minutes in boiling water, then drain. Mix with the olive oil marinade, prepared with the parsley, garlic, pinch of salt, cumin and lemon juice. Serve warm or cold.

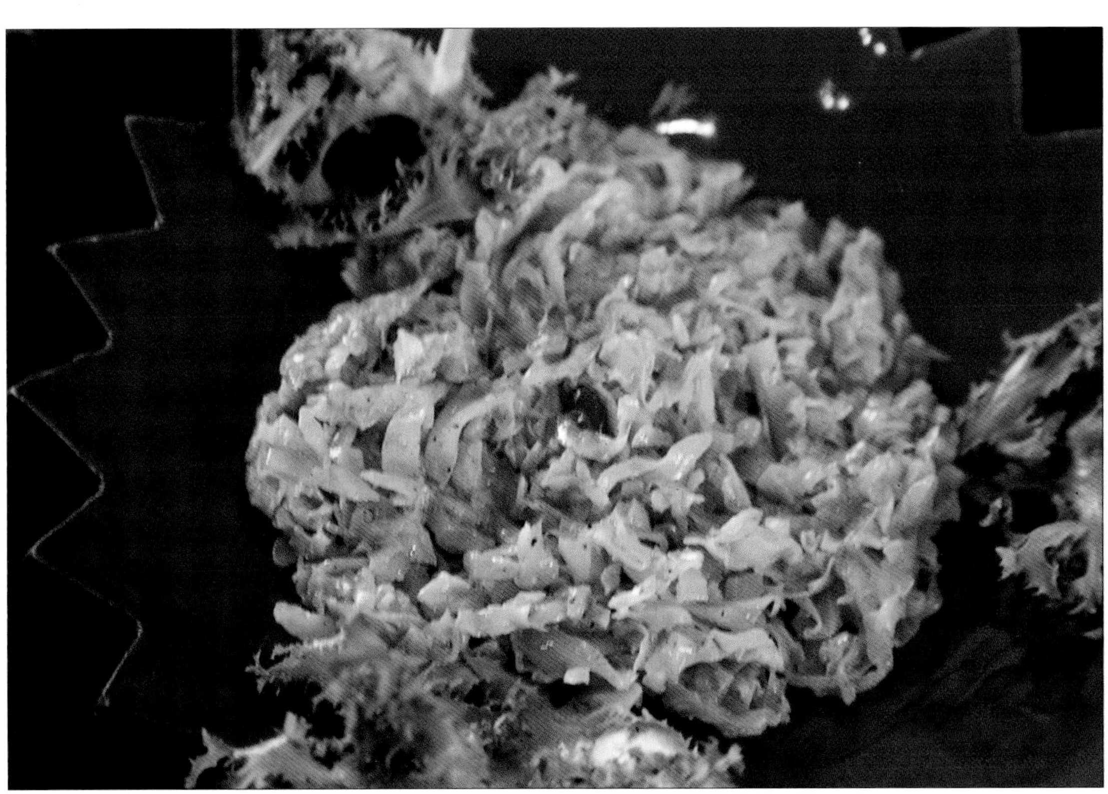

# Taktuka salad (recipe from The Maison Arabe)

## with red and green peppers

**Ingredients for 2 servings**

- 2 large green peppers,
- 2 tomatoes,
- 3 cloves garlic,
- 2 tablespoons olive oil,
- 1 teaspoon paprika,
- 1 teaspoon cumin,
- 1 teaspoon salt,
- 1 teaspoon black pepper,
- 2 bouquets parsley.

Cut the tomatoes into small cubes and mix them with the oil, crushed garlic cloves, ground parsley, salt, cumin, paprika and pepper. Cut the peppers into strips and grill them lightly, then add them to the rest of the ingredients and cook over a low heat for around fifteen minutes. Garnish the plate with slices of tomato and an olive. Serve warm or cold.

# Carrot purée with lemon (recipe from The Maison Arabe)

**Ingredients for 2 servings**

- 500 g carrots,
- 2 bouquets parsley,
- 1 teaspoon cumin,
- 1 teaspoon paprika,
- 1 teaspoon salt,
- 1 teaspoon pepper,
- 1/2 teaspoon strong chilli powder,
- 1 tablespoon lemon juice,
- 3 chopped cloves garlic.

Soften the carrots in boiling water, then drain and cook in oil for 15 minutes over a low heat, adding the ground parsley, cumin, paprika, salt, pepper, garlic, chilli powder and lemon juice. Garnish the plate with round slices of lemon, and serve warm or cold.

# Aubergine purée (recipe from The Maison Arabe)

**Ingredients for 2 servings**

- 4 medium-sized aubergines,
- 4 tomatoes,
- 4 cloves garlic,
- 2 tablespoons sunflower or peanut oil,
- 1 teaspoon paprika,
- 1 teaspoon cumin,
- 1 teaspoon salt,
- 1 teaspoon chilli powder,
- 2 bouquets parsley.

Cut the aubergines into large dice and fry in the sunflower oil, then drain. During this time, cut the tomatoes into quarters, remove the part with the seeds, cut the remainder into small dice and place all of the above into a frying pan with the salt, ground parsley, garlic and spices. Cook over a low heat, continuing to stir until a thick sauce is obtained. Crush the aubergines in a bowl with a wooden spatula, add the tomato purée and cook the mixture for around 2 minutes before flambeing with the lemon juice. Garnish with an olive and a few lettuce leaves.
Serve hot or cold (according to taste).

# Egg *kefta* (recipe from Riad Laksour)

*Kefta* is minced meat which is used for stuffing food such as briouats, but also forms the basis of other dishes, generally cooked in a *tagine* (ceramic pot), as is the case for this recipe.

**Ingredients for 2-4 servings**

- 500g minced meat,
- 150g butter,
- 1 bouquet ground parsley,
- 2 teaspoons mild chilli powder,
- 1 teaspoon cumin,
- 1 teaspoon coriander,
- 1 pinch pepper or strong chilli powder,
- salt,
- 4 eggs,
- 1 onion.

Mix the mincemeat, stirring in the parsley, the finely-chopped onion, salt and spices, then make it into tiny balls. Cook in a frying pan with the butter without adding water and leave the meat to soak, then turn the heat down. Avoid stirring too much, and you will obtain a creamy sauce, coloured by the mild chilli powder. Reduce heat and wait until mealtime before finishing off. A few minutes before serving, move the meat and sauce into a tagine and apply a low heat. When the sauce starts to simmer, break the eggs into the mixture, sprinkle them with salt and wait until the whites are cooked before removing the tagine from the heat.

# Méchoui (recipe from Riad Laksour)

**Ingredients for 8 servings**

- 3 kg shoulder or side of mutton,
- 1 tablespoon mild chilli powder,
- 1 teaspoon cumin,
- 100g butter,
- salt.

Coat the meat with the butter and spice mix and cook in the oven for approximately four hours, turning it midway through cooking and occasionally sprinkling with a glass of water to stop it from drying out. Before removing from the oven, check that it has a good golden colour and comes away easily. Put the meat on a dish that can be decorated with vegetables (boiled carrot roundels, potatoes, turnips, etc., with just a touch of salt). Put small hors-d'œuvres dishes of cumin, pepper and salt on the table; guests will "dip" their meat pieces in these to enhance the taste still further.

# Prune tagine (recipe from Riad Laksour)

**Ingredients for 4-6 servings**

- 1.5 kg loin or shoulder of lamb (or mutton; alternatively, 2 chickens cut into pieces if needed),
- 500 g prunes,
- 1 tablespoon grilled sesame seeds,
- 200 g almonds,
- 1 teaspoon pepper,
- 1/2 teaspoon saffron,
- 1 stick cinnamon,
- 1 teaspoon powdered cinnamon,
- 2 grated onions,
- 200 g butter,
- 4 tablespoons sugar (which may be replaced by honey if desired),
- 4 tablespoons olive oil.

Cut the meat into pieces and place in a pressure cooker, adding the salt, pepper, saffron, cinnamon stick, grated onions and butter. Cover and cook over a low heat, adding 2 large glasses of water. Turn the pieces from time to time, and pour in a little additional water during cooking if necessary. When the skin comes away easily, remove the meat from the heat and add the prunes. After fifteen minutes' cooking, add the cinnamon and sugar (or honey), and then reduce until you are left with a sauce which is not too thick. Check the seasoning and replace the meat in the pan, without crushing the prunes, then remove from the heat.

Blanch the almonds before frying them in olive oil for a few minutes.

Add this mixture to the meat, and place in a *tagine* (ceramic pot), then simmer over a low heat for around fifteen minutes before serving. Garnish the dish with the sesame seeds.

# Tagine Royal (or multifruits) (recipe from The Maison Arabe)

**Ingredients for 2-4 servings, depending on the number of courses in the meal**

- 500 g lamb cut into pieces, or 1 chicken (using the thighs and white meat), or 500 g beef,
- 1 bowl olive oil,
- 1 tablespoon salt,
- 1 teaspoon pepper,
- 1 tablespoon sugar,
- 1 teaspoon powdered cinnamon,
- 1 stick cinnamon,
- 1/2 teaspoon saffron,
- 2 teaspoons *ras el hanout*, a mixture of many spices (Moroccan grocers sell ready-made mixes which can include up to thirty or so different ingredients, including ginger and turmeric),
- a dozen dates, twenty hulled almonds,
- a dozen dried apricots, a handful of raisins, a dozen dried figs,
- a handful of nuts, a dozen prunes,
- a tablespoon of sesame seeds.

Simmer (ideally in a terracotta *tagine* pot) the lamb (or beef, or chicken pieces) for at least one hour in a sauce consisting of a little water, olive oil, salt, pepper, cinnamon, saffron and the spice mix. A few minutes before the end of cooking, caramelise the mixture slightly by adding the sugar.

During this time, simmer the dried figs, prunes and apricots over a low heat for a few minutes in a sugar syrup flavoured with the cinnamon stick, caramelising them slightly. Also split open the dates, remove their stones and replace with an almond.

After cooking, cover the meat (retaining the sauce) with the fruits, laying them out in quarters (1/4 stuffed dates, 1/4 figs, 1/4 prunes and 1/4 apricots). Garnish the food (still in quarters) with the sesame seeds (on the prunes), almonds (on the dates), raisins (on the apricots) and nuts (on the figs). Cover the tagine with its lid and simmer everything for a last few minutes before serving the dish, accompanied with bread.

# Berber or vegetable couscous

(recipe from Dar Ayniwen and Riad Laksour)

**Ingredients for 2-3 servings**

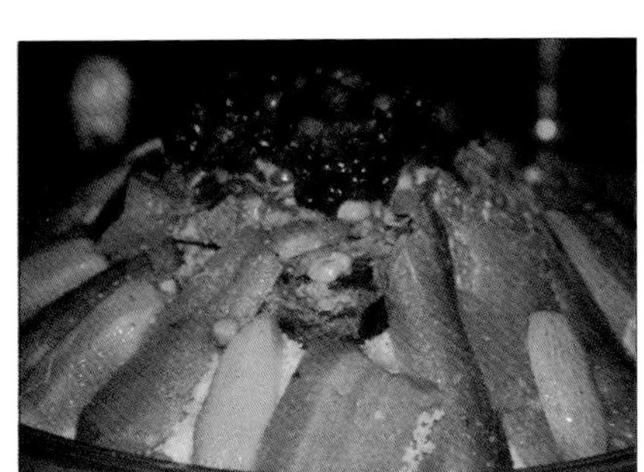

- 2 chopped turnips,
- 3 carrots halved lengthways,
- 3 onions cut into rings,
- 2 courgettes halved lengthways,
- 3 halved tomatoes,
- 1 teaspoon pepper,
- 1 tablespoon salt,
- 1 tablespoon ground parsley,
- 1 bowl olive oil,
- 1/2 teaspoon saffron,
- 1 litre water (to cover the vegetables in the pan),
- 2 shoulders lamb.

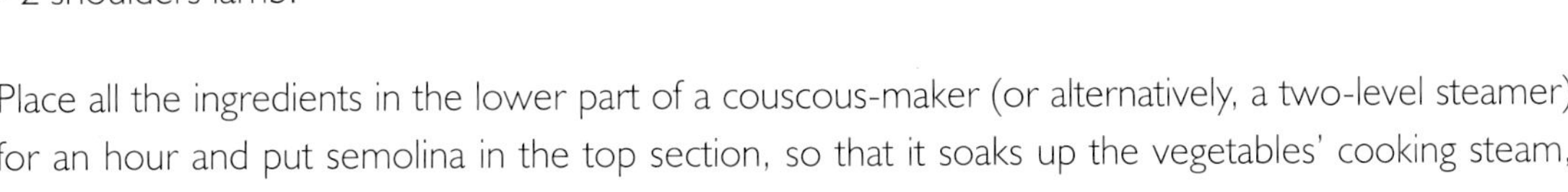

Place all the ingredients in the lower part of a couscous-maker (or alternatively, a two-level steamer) for an hour and put semolina in the top section, so that it soaks up the vegetables' cooking steam, adding to its aroma.

When the vegetables are ready, lay out the semolina in the middle of the plate, making a small hollow into which the meat is then placed. Cover the food with the vegetables.

To make the dish more attractive, Habiba, the Riad Laksour's dada, arranges carrots and courgettes in alternation and by order of height, topping the dish off at the last minute with onions which have been pre-caramelised with sugar, in a pan, a few minutes before serving...

# Milk *pastilla* (recipe from Riad Laksour)

**Ingredients for 2 servings**

- 1.5 litre milk,
- 4 tablespoons rice powder,
- 1 small glass orange blossom water (optional),
- 50g butter,
- 250g ground almonds,
- 20 lumps sugar,
- 30 *ouarka* sheets,
- cooking oil.

Preparation of *ouarka* sheets

- 500g sieved durum wheat flour,
- 500g fine sieved flour,
- 1 teaspoon salt.

Make a dough with the initial consistency of a bread dough. Knead firmly, without damaging its elasticity, adding a little water from time to time until a supple, soft dough is obtained. Work it by lifting and then striking on the table. Next, dampen your fingers, take a little dough and strike it several times against a hot pancake griddle. This repeated action will leave spots of dough on the griddle, which will form a sort of ultrafine pancake as they heat up. Repeat the process until you have the number of sheets you need. Stack them on a plate to cool, then cover with a cloth. As this recipe requires plenty of dexterity and patience, you may be able to buy ready-made sheets if you are lucky enough to find a Moroccan bakery, but they will probably not be as fine (to prevent them from being broken during transport, the bakers prefer to make the "pancakes" a little thicker to improve their strength). Alternatively, buy rolls of ready-made flaky pastry from a hypermarket, and roll them as flat as possible with a rolling pin…

Preparation of the milk sauce

Boil the milk with the sugar, then add the rice powder, orange blossom water (optional) and butter. Thicken, but not too much, then remove the mixture from the heat and leave to cool. Put the ground almonds into a little boiling oil, add 1/2 (small) glass of caster sugar, then remove the mixture from the heat.

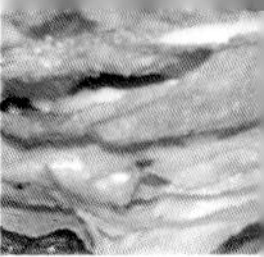



### Preparation of the dessert

Cut the *ouarka* sheets into circles and brown them, two at a time, in a pan of boiling oil, then drain. Thirty minutes before serving, put the sheets into the oven on a low heat for 15 minutes. Next, place the sheets three at a time on a large plate, sprinkle with the almond powder and cover with two other sheets, onto which the milk sauce is then poured. Repeat this process several times to obtain a stack of "stuffed" sheets. Pour a final layer of milk over the top, and garnish with powdered cinnamon if desired.

This is a very light dessert, and fairly refreshing if the milk sauce is left in the refrigerator for at least 30 minutes before serving…

# *Useful information*

## In the Medina

**Riad 72**
Tel.: 00-212-44-431900.
Fax: 00-212-44-431786.
E-mail: riadomaroc@iam.net.ma
Website: www.riadomaroc.com
From 91 to 335 euros per room per night, including Moroccan breakfast.

**Riad Zina**
38, Derb Assabane, Riad Laarouss, Medina.
Tel./fax: 00-212-44-385242.
E-mail: riadzina@iam.net.ma
Website: www.riadzina.ma
From 1000 to 2000 dirhams per room or suite per night, including breakfast.

**Riad Laksour**
Tel.: 00-212-44-431900.
Fax: 00-212-44-431786.
E-mail: riadomaroc@iam.net.ma
Website: www.riadomaroc.com
From 53 to 114 euros per night, depending on room or suite, in all seasons, Moroccan breakfast included. Hire of whole riad: 407 euros per night.

**Villa des Orangers**
6, rue Sidi Mimoun.
Tel.: 00-212-44-384638.
Fax: 00-212-44-385123.
E-mail: message@villadesorangers.com
Website: www.villadesorangers.com
From 2800 to 4500 dirhams per room or suite.

**Dar Moha**
81, rue Dar El Bacha.
Tel.: 00-212-44-386400.
Fax: 00-212-44-386998.
E-mail: darmoha@iam.net.ma
Website: www.darmoha.ma
From 1000 to 1500 dirhams per room per night, including breakfast.

**Riad Loubna**
Tel.: 00-212-44-431900.
Fax : 00-212-44-431786.
E-mail: riadomaroc@iam.net.ma
Website: www.riadomaroc.com
From 91 to 335 euros per room per night, Moroccan breakfast included. Hire of whole riad: from 381 to 419 euros per day.

**Riad Habib**
Tel.: 00-212-44 431900.
Fax : 00-212-44 431786.
E-mail: riadomaroc@iam.net.ma
Website: www.riadomaroc.com
From 14 to 51 euros per room or suite per night, Moroccan breakfast included. Hire of whole riad: from 693 to 722 euros per day or from 4360 to 4573 euros per week, depending on number of occupants and season.

**Riad Laïla**
Tel.: 00-212-44 431900.
Fax: 00-212-44 431786.
E-mail: riadomaroc@iam.net.ma
Website: www.riadomaroc.com
Hire of whole riad for one week: from 3049 to 5255 euros, depending on the season and the number of guests occupying the rooms (maximum 15-18). Over Christmas and New Year, add 50 % to the highest price. Room hire (price per room per night for 1-3 guests, including breakfast): from 114 to 225 euros.

**Riad Mabrouka**
Tel.: 00-212-44-431900.
Fax: 00-212-44- 431786.
E-mail: riadomaroc@iam.net.ma
Website: www.riadomaroc.com
From 133 to 1970 euros per room per night, Moroccan breakfast included. From 725 to 799 euros per night for the whole riad (around 5800 euros per week).

**The Maison Arabe**
1, Derb Assehbé,
Bab Doukkala.
Tel.: 00-212-44-387010.
Fax: 00-212-44-387221.
E-mail: maisonarabe@iam.net.ma
Website: www.lamaisonarabe.com
From 1700 to 6000 dirhams per room or suite, per night, including breakfast.

## In the Palmery

**Jnane Tamsna**
Douar Abiab,
The Palmery.
Fax: 00-212-44 329884.
E-mail: info@tamsna.com
Website: www.tamsna.com
From 350 euros per room, which includes breakfast, use of the swimming pool, the tennis court, transfers to/from airport, limitless soft drinks, tea, coffee and home-made pâtisserie. For half-board (the meals are excellent): 430 euros, all drinks included (wines and apéritifs), per room.

**Dar Ayniwen**
Palmery "Circuit".
Tel.: 00-212-44-329684/85.
Fax: 00-212-44-329686.
E-mail: infos@dar-ayniwen.com
Website: www.dar-ayniwen.com
From around 3300 to 5400 dirhams per room, suite or house per night, depending on season. Breakfast is included. Hire of the entire villa: around 115,000-150,000 dirhams per week, for 8 guests staying half-board.

**Caravan Serai**
264, Ouled Ben Rahmoun,
The Palmery.
Tel.: 00-212-44-300302.
Fax: 00-212-44-300262.
E-mail: caravanserai@iam.net.ma
Website:
www.caravanserai-marrakesh.com
From 700 to 3750 dirhams per room or suite per night, breakfast included.

**Les Deux Tours**
Palmery "Circuit".
Tel.: 00-212-44-329527/26/25.
Fax: 00-212-44-329523.
E-mail: deuxtours@iam.net.ma
Website: www.deux-tours.com
Between 1750 and 3000 dirhams per room or suite.

## Moroccan Tourist Office

**Marrakech**
Tourist Office
170, avenue Mohamed V
Tel.: 00-212-44-430886
Fax: 00-212-44-436057

## Short glossary

**Bouhou:** external salon, generally in the shade of the patio arcades.

**Dar:** house or group of houses, broadly speaking.

**Douirrya:** small house adjoining a dar or riad, for which it generally acts as an extension.

**Gap:** dried and chiselled plaster. Generally used to decorate arcades and ceilings; very lace-like.

**Khettaras:** subterranean irrigation channels.

**Medersa:** Koranic school.

**Medina:** old town, including the mosque and the souks.

**Mellah:** Jewish quarter.

**Riad:** patio garden around which the house or palace is centred. By extension, the word also refers to a very specific type of house with a patio, or even an entire quarter previously made up of several such residences.

**Tadelakt:** smooth wall coating made from a mixture of coloured lime and soft soap. Initially spread by hand using a spatula, it is left to dry, then smoothed and polished with a flat stone before being waxed (egg whites were used in the past) and polished again to a brilliant sheen. Although the application of a tadlakt coating to a wall is a physically arduous and rather painstaking job, it will provide lasting protection against damp – an inevitable problem in the Medina, despite the ambient heat. This traditional procedure has become a genuine fashion phenomenon, particularly since the coloured pigments added to the lime can often produce very attractive colour gradations which add to a room's atmosphere.

**Zellij:** decorative enamelled ceramics, generally produced from small, multicoloured geometric pieces which combine to form a sort of mosaic placed on floors, tables, walls, columns, etc.

## *Bibliography*


- *Morocco* - Insight Guides, APA Publications, 2001.
- *Morocco* - Lonely Planet, Lonely Planet Publications, Jan 1998.
- *The Rough Guide to Morocco* - Mark Ellingham, Don Grisbrook & Shaun Mc Veigh, Rough Guides Ltd, April 2001.
- *Morocco* - Blue Guide, A & C Black Limited, May 1998.
- *Morocco* - NEOS Guide, Michelin Travel Publications, 2001.



This work was produced the graphics department
(under the direction of Isabelle Gérard) by Renaissance International.

Printed by Milanostampa (CE).
Legal Deposit : February 2003 ; D/2003/8176/470.